'David Martin writes engagingly and with humility. He unflinchingly points out some of our blindspots – the areas where we might be absorbing the values of our culture instead of challenging its accepted norms.'

Cara Fitzpatrick, housewife and trainer for Precept Ministries Ireland

'What if our indulgence in a certain thing or ideology was really only making us less happy and more dull? Insightful and to-the-point, David Martin diagnoses some root causes of our spiritual anemia. You may be surprised, alarmed, or annoyed to see yourself illustrated in the pages of this book. But not to worry, the author delivers the remedy we all need. Take up and read!'

Gloria Furman, author of Missional Motherhood *and* Labor with Hope

'This book is the equivalent of a literary defibrillator that will reignite our hearts to beat and long for all that eternity will afford. David Martin has penned a spiritual alarm clock that will stop us sleepwalking distractedly into eternity with our gaze consumed by temporal nothingness. This book exhorts us to be different, it is brilliantly written and ubiquitously needed.'

Jonathan Gemmell, The Proclamation Trust

'In this pithy and punchy book, David Martin helps us look at our world and at ourselves and to seek to be more godly. It's worth reading prayerfully.'

Peter Jensen, Former Archbishop of Sydney

D1328984

'David Martin fearlessly puts his finger on many of the prevailing faults in our contemporary Christian lifestyles and calls Christians to dare to be different to the prevailing culture.'

Jeremy Marshall, businessman and evangelist

'David challenges and encourages us to be in every way true disciples of Jesus in a world, and indeed a church, that needs men and women to step into this calling. I found this book a real challenge and encouragement in my own call to be a disciple of Jesus. An excellent book and a real gift to the church at this time.'

David McClay, Rector of Willowfield Church, Belfast, Archdeacon of Down Diocese and Chairperson of New Wine Ireland

'This hard-hitting book is a timely and powerful reminder of the truth that we are a new creation in Christ, created to be shockingly, beautifully, starkly different from the world around us. Be challenged, encouraged and rebuked – before turning your face in joy and thanksgiving to Christ and his powerful work to redeem his people even despite his people!'

Steve Timmis, CEO Acts 29

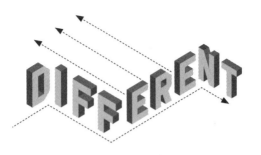

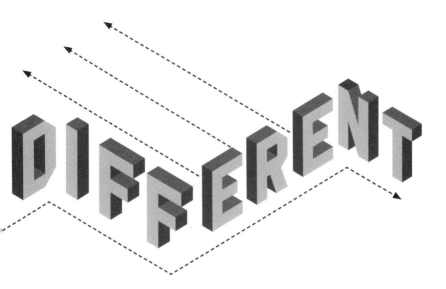

DIFFERENT

Our witness and the sins
that work against it

DAVID MARTIN

10 Publishing
a division of 10 **of those** .com

Copyright © 2019 by David Martin

First published in Great Britain in 2019

British Library Cataloguing in Publication Data
A record for this book is available from the British Library

ISBN: 978-1-912373-60-4

Designed by Jude May

Printed in Denmark by Nørhaven

10Publishing, a division of 10ofthose.com
Unit C, Tomlinson Road, Leyland, PR25 2DY, England
Email: info@10ofthose.com
Website: www.10ofthose.com

For Honor, the greatest earthly blessing, fellow pilgrim and best evidence of God's constant grace, love and encouragement I know.

Contents

Introduction

This is a book about *nothing*. It is about *nothing* in the same sense that children use the word when caught doing *something* they know they ought not to be. Their 'nothing' is really code for 'something' they know will get them into trouble, yet they want every adult to think that really it *is* nothing at all. Similarly, this book is about some important issues we would prefer everyone else to think are nothing, in the hope that we can continue doing what we really want. It highlights the more imperceptible sins that Christians in the Western world are particularly prone to in the early twenty-first century.

Before you perhaps dismiss me for getting all self-righteous, I am as every bit imperfect, wilfully disobedient and sinful as anyone else. I am simply a fellow traveller, undeservingly destined for heaven and sustained daily by the abundant and overflowing grace of my great God and Saviour Jesus Christ. What follows then is, of course, an imperfect reaction to these sins.

There are many challenges that every Christian has to face in today's popular culture. Some are facing these pressures forthrightly and in the public square. Political causes such as the LGBTQ (Lesbian, Gay, Bisexual, Transgender/Transsexual and Queer) worldview, abortion and euthanasia all deserve carefully nuanced and brave responses. Yet many advocates among such causes look at the church today and, perhaps rightly, accuse it of missing the plank in its own eye. When the world can see legitimate grounds for not listening to the church as it speaks about such things as sexual immorality, then by its own standards the church must seriously take stock.

I of course don't mean that Christians should stand idly by until we dot every biblical 'i' and cross all our doctrinal 't's, saying nothing to culture. Our very understanding of sanctification compels us to be the first to admit that we are not yet the finished product. Where a deep understanding of grace exists in the church, it will always speak from a humbled position. The church is comprised of those who know they are fallen and yet have taken God's offer of forgiveness. Christians should not therefore be slow or embarrassed in crying out for godly repentance and faith, both within their own ranks and outside them as well.

Nevertheless, to go on without listening to the world's responses is surely to shoot ourselves in the foot – theologically, socially and culturally. Therefore one of the most pressing issues confronting us in our engagement with culture and our efforts in evangelism is our own credibility: our credibility as those who ought to be not only enjoying God's good but broken creation here and now, but more importantly focusing on the world that is yet to come. The main burden of this book then is a concern that today's Western Christians worry far more about our credit-ability than we do about our credibility. We worry about our financial, social or own personal emotional capital, while all the time not realising that our spiritual, holy and eternal capital is suffering as a result.

Putting this as a question might help: don't Christians today spend an inordinate amount of thought on the things of this world, leaving precious little time to prepare for something far more significant? I worry that our delight in God, through Jesus Christ and by the power of the Spirit, is so anaemic. Given this, no one would ever dare even contemplate becoming a Christian, for all they see is a spiritualised veneer of their own lives as they already are. Why bother becoming a Christian if doing so simply means trying to pretend that you are interested in God and eternity, when in reality your interests lie in this world and the best it has to offer? God would be an accoutrement at best, an inconvenience at worst. There is nothing attractive, compelling, never mind biblical about that – at all.

The topics under scrutiny here are by no means exhaustive. They are, however, ancient and therefore worthy of our consideration. They are the perennial problems that every generation of Christian pilgrims must tackle anew. In this sense, then, I am not intentionally setting out to say anything novel. Rather, I am continuing Moses' tradition of telling God's people to repeatedly remind themselves about the law of the Lord. Interestingly, Moses repeatedly reminded the Israelites of the need to do this not because of the dangers of poverty, but because of the threat that prosperity would pose in the Promised Land (Deut. 6:10–15; 8:6–20; 28:47; 32:15).

Perhaps you will read this and think there really is nothing in it at all. For a large majority of Christians in the world, if they were even able to afford this book, they would not recognise the problems. They live with poverty, face regular persecution and prize heaven far above their few meagre worldly possessions. This book would miss the mark completely for them. However, there are pseudo-gospels preached in such countries that do promise these very things I'm debunking and overthrowing. Such health, wealth and prosperity gospels are as out of place in the Bible's story as a champion hotdog eater would be in a local vegan support group.

Alternatively, as you read this, you might ponder whether there is just something in it. For those of you who have already flexed your credit-ability to buy the book, you'll need to decide for yourselves.

1

Materialism:
Caravans and the Exodus

Coffee, cars and caravans

I was sitting in my 'office' (aka the best coffee shop in the local area), drinking my 'coffee' (aka my painstakingly blended work of art, called a flat white). As I sat working on next Sunday's sermon, my attention was drawn by a man trying to get his newly purchased, oversized, ultra-HD plasma screen, smart TV into his undersized, newly purchased, eco-friendly, electric-powered, emissions-reducing Smart car! I was suddenly struck that before my eyes was a picture of the struggle that modern people face: to squeeze more and more into our increasingly compact world.

In this struggle we feel we are at least somebody! In the effort to squeeze more and more into our ever increasingly compact world, we think that at least proves we have the purchasing power to do so. 'What a joke,' I thought to myself – from my self-assured, superior vantage point, sipping my rapidly cooling cup of glorified caffeine, typing on my trusty iGod (aka a MacBook Pro).

Different

Admittedly, a coffee shop is not the best place to have an 'office'. Mine is in the middle of a shopping complex where I can witness the same act of consumerism being played out multiple times in an hour. Yet at the very same time I am uncritically engaging in my own incessant thirst for more. As my coffee house has Wi-Fi, with the simple click of a button I can enter a global megastore where digital shelves are overflowing with products that generally I have absolutely no use for, but apparently I need. A brief search on my Amazon history alone proves that over the course of a year I have been almost oblivious to my attempts to squeeze more and more into my supposedly already Spirit-filled Christian life.

My experience in ministry thus far has confirmed that I am not alone in this. I am actually tempted to venture that it is one of the most dangerous, even fatal, sicknesses that is currently plaguing the church in my own part of the world: Northern Ireland. Regardless of how much we say, and no matter how much we do, when we retreat to our well-furnished, amply provided for lifestyles, it dangerously compromises the power, hope and substance of our message.

For example, I was completely shocked and totally unprepared for my first summer, in 2016, as an official employee of the Church of Ireland. I had had plenty of ministry experience up until then among an inner-city, international, young, vibrant church. I had finished two theology degrees and read enough Puritan literature to feel confident that even though I had not seen every sin imaginable, at least I would be ready for it. But then, to finish my training, I was moved to a respectable, affluent, very comfortable parish. 'What on earth could happen there?' I thought! While the first nine months went swimmingly, though with the same old problems that arise in any ministry, out of nowhere I was confronted with one of the dangers of prosperity. With the onset of summer, the church suddenly shrunk. The bustling children's ministry almost evaporated. The car park was actually useable. The bums on pews were afforded plenty of space. And there was an eerie feeling of irrelevancy that descended over the church. Yet the most troubling part of all was its acceptability: being absent from church, not just for two or three weeks but for the entire summer, was simply something that many people did at this time of the year, didn't they?

When I talk about the exodus, I should think back with utter amazement at the powerful working of Almighty God. He conquered the oppressive Egyptian army and delivered his people out of slavery, bringing them into the Promised Land flowing with milk and honey. Instead, I think of that multitude of vehicles disappearing over the horizon as Christians in their droves disengaged from their church family. They hitched their newly acquired, super-deluxe, solar-powered, extendable, convertible caravan to their superbly shining, newly valeted SUV. Sadly, I'm not exaggerating here, and all this was done without batting an eyelid about how odd this pursuit of worldly things is for Christians destined, one day, to arrive in heaven in glory.

Culture wars

It is well documented and acknowledged by many thinking Christians today that 'culture' is difficult to define because it is almost impossible to detect the culture in which you are living. It is simply the air we breathe; the water we depend on; the norms and values that we assume and reinforce by participating in everyday life.

The local church must live in its culture while being distinctive. This requires a continual critical assessment of its own culture – a tricky and demanding exercise. It must be in the world but not of the world. It must seek to win the world by both affirming what is good and at the very same time condemning what is bad. A church earnestly engaging with its surrounding culture in this way will be noted as being full of grace and yet seasoned with salt. This is part of the mission of every Christian and any faithful church.

The danger is that, perhaps over time, a church can unthinkingly and imperceptibly absorb the values and attitudes of the very culture it was initially trying to challenge and change. The dangerous and pervasive spirit of materialism has suffused itself so successfully into the life of the church that no one seems to worry about it any longer. In this regard we are just like everyone else.

Famously Gordon Gekko pronounced, 'Greed is good'. The church laughs along with its secular neighbour at the crudity of the statement, but in reality we can easily believe either that greed is one of those 'minor' sins that doesn't do anyone that much harm, or that it is a sin we personally are not guilty of committing.

But what of our desire to keep up with the Joneses? Why our insatiable thirst for the latest, must-have phones, watches, tablets and so on? Where does our underlying grumpiness and persistent dissatisfaction with life come from? And why do we find all these things so easy to excuse in ourselves, simply because everyone else is doing it?

Keeping the faith

I must be careful not to fall under the strong condemnation

of 1 Timothy 4:1–5 at this point. In an attempt to prove their superior spiritual position, some people were troubling the church in Ephesus with teaching that 'forbid people to marry and order[ed] them to abstain from certain foods' (v. 3). Yet Paul instructs Timothy that such a prohibition is the teaching of demons – God's creation is good and to be enjoyed. Marriage and food (two things which I wholeheartedly support) are held up as evidence of the skilful, wise and immensely diverse creativity of God. He made them 'to be received with thanksgiving by those who believe and know the truth'.

In other words, Christians are not to be seen by culture as those who avoid the richness of God's creation. The fine taste of a perfectly cooked steak; the full-bodied flavour of a glass of merlot; the joy of love; the warmth of an embrace between a husband and wife; the great outdoors, where God's power can be experienced first-hand; the solace of life-long friendships; dare I even mention that initial early morning buzz that caffeine delivers – all these things, along with a trillion other experiences, have come from the infinitely creative and loving heart of a good and generous God. They are not to be shunned or avoided but are, with thankfulness, to be used and celebrated in a way that pleases their Maker.

However, in that very same letter Paul has to warn Timothy too not to chase after the things of this world and especially personal wealth. 'Those who want to get rich fall into temptation and a trap and into many foolish and harmful desires that plunge men into ruin and destruction. For the love of money is a root of all kinds of evil. Some people, eager for money, have wandered away from the faith and pierced themselves with many griefs' (1 Tim. 6:9–10). This is a healthy corrective to our unhealthy obsessions. Though written almost

2000 years ago, Paul's word could be an editorial piece for the *Financial Times* warning about the psychological, emotional, physical and above all spiritual power that we attach to money, and that can destroy us in all those ways.

In the very same year that I watched in disbelief as countless Christians disappeared over the horizon for most of the summer, I also experienced the tragic sharp edge of Paul's teaching on the love of money. Jeff (an alias) had arrived at my church completely depressed. His back story was a series of tragic events, but as he himself admitted they all issued from his relentless desire to be rich. He took a punt with his life savings, his family home and numerous loans from his extended family. He then lost absolutely everything. He also lost the patience of everyone who knew him and the trust of those he loved. They did love him, but he had become too toxic to be around as he tried to salvage his dreams of being wealthy. His pursuit of money plunged him into ruin and destruction. As church resumed its autumn schedule, I got a phone call one night to inform me that he had committed suicide.

Please note that it is the *love* of money that is Paul's main concern here. Money in and of itself is neither good nor bad. A certain amount is necessary for living today – poverty is a terrible thing. But neither is being rich necessarily wrong. Some people are born 'into money', or have the natural ability to make lots of it. Others are blessed by people's generosity. Paul's writing is very careful. He has already said that we are to enjoy God's good creation and in 1 Timothy 6 acknowledges that it is perfectly possible to be rich and still live as a real Christian. But what he so forcefully does is to call us all to wake up to the nature of our own hearts. They are built to love, so if we are not loving one thing, we will inexorably be driven to love something else. Money is particularly attractive to the desires and longings of all our hearts. This is why if you are poor, money seems to be the answer, and if you are rich, it still seems to be the answer to the dissatisfaction that lies deep within.

This love of money demonstrates itself in a multitude of ways. Very often it is by acquiring more and more things. It can prompt the Facebook posts and Instagram snaps of our latest must-have experiences. It may cause us to associate with new friends because, like them, we can now afford to shop, dine or holiday with the in-crowd.

What we do with our money and how it affects us is a concern. No one can argue that the Bible's teaching on money is irrelevant today. I need to hear such warnings almost on a daily basis. I am far happier to stay in the territory of 1 Timothy 4 where I can comfort myself that by entering into the kaleidoscopic fullness of all that there is to be enjoyed in this world, then at least I am not in danger of promoting the teaching of demons. It is far more complicated and demanding to work out carefully and regularly when my heart is beginning to chase after and be defined by my money or lack thereof.

Could anyone say that you are different from the accepted norms of the world you currently inhabit simply because you are a Christian? To return to my previous example, instead of checking out of your church family for the summer and taking refuge in the comfort of your caravan, chalet or cruise ship, could you actually prioritise being in your church in the holiday months? That sounds like a small and almost inconsequential thing, but in practice it would be a monumental shift for many people. Not only would it teach your heart a valuable lesson, but it would be an example to many others as well. You would be saying, 'Yes, I love my holidays. I need time away from the norm simply to look after my body and mental health. At the same time, however, I don't want to miss being fed the spiritual food of God's word. I need that even more and feel the worse for missing it.' Of course some people will protest and say that they go to other churches when they are away. I'm glad they are going to a church somewhere. However, a long-term vacation from your home church – except for genuine reasons such as a short-term mission or ill health – betrays a low view that the people and relationships there are not worth the sacrifice of precious holiday time. This might appear an overstatement, but it is what we do with the time that is really ours that shows us where our hearts truly are. When term time is in full swing, we can simply be carried along by the commitments that demand our time. But when we are free to spend our time as we like, we see where our true commitments lie. If we don't 'have to be' at church, will we still delight to be there? Those who chose to 'take a break' from their church and 'visit' other churches also demonstrate a low view of them. At worst it is spiritual foraging in someone else's field with no intention of contributing long-term to the life of that church. Such 'touring' Christians are in league with those students who church-hop during their university years, consuming a pick-and-mix diet of spiritual sound bites.

You may be thinking that I've gone overboard here. In some sense I'm looking for exactly this reaction, and it proves that I am challenging a cultural norm. I can hear some people say, 'I don't know what David has gotten all worked up over. After all we are only talking about going to church.' But that is precisely my point. Rather than discussing *going to* church, we are addressing what church means and how that should change our attitude towards it.

The church is not simply a social club that meets the interests of a select few in any particular community. Neither is the church the property of any small group of people with membership cards and voting rights. It is not an alternative source of entertainment, a platform for a political party or person, or a hobby for a few enthusiasts and a take-it-or-leave-it option for your average Christian. The church is the clearest sign to the world that Jesus has indeed been raised from the dead and that all who truly trust in him are destined for glory (Col. 1:18). The church is the unavoidable demonstration of where the history of the entire world is headed, as it willingly submits to Jesus' lordship today (Eph. 1:10). The regular meeting of your local church is the best place to hear and apply the gracious word of the living God (Heb. 12:18–24). The church is what matters most to Jesus (John 21:15–19). The church is the light of the world and the salt of the earth (Matt. 5:13–16). To think that any human or group of people might have sole ownership and control of the church is surely a mistake. To have a casual and easy relationship with the church is worse. If your relationship with your church and with the people in your church has no claim on you, your resources and your time, then something is wrong somewhere.

Jesus gives a very clear warning: if there is no (or even just a minor) difference between you and the rest of the world in how you view your financial capital and what you do with your time, Jesus will be hard pushed to recognise you on the ultimate pay day. His 'salty' words are exactly what we need to hear (Matt. 5:13).

A matter of trust

As I mentioned before, the danger for the Israelites in the Promised Land was not from poverty but from prosperity.

23

Achan felt the full weight of this warning when he tried accruing for himself some of the trinkets of the other nations (Josh. 7). The same is seen in the New Testament where Ananias and Sapphira tried pretending to be fully invested in the progress of the kingdom when actually they wanted to live with a foot in both worlds (Acts 5). These stories and others repeat the same point: you cannot love both God and money.

The clarion call of this book is to ask who you actually are prepared to trust. This is something that is played out in family homes again and again. Children get annoyed with their parents, they shout and argue, they lie and deceive, they even disobey and do the opposite to what they are being told to do. I've been wrestling with this for some time now with one of our four children. Then I read Paul Tripp's book *Parenting: 14 Gospel Principles That Can Radically Change Your Family* (Crossway Books, 2016). I was struck by how he drew attention to the importance of speaking to our children's hearts. That is where the real problem lies, which as parents we dare not miss. Changing actions may work for a while, but what we should be seeking to address is their attitudes. In applying Tripp's thesis to the bedrock of all the other anti-social problems in my child's behaviour, I saw it to be a matter of trust.

Why do our children shout and lie and disobey? Why do they question, argue over and constantly push the boundaries? And why are parents exhausted, worried and perplexed at the end of another day by the seemingly unchanging actions of their children? The tactic my wife and I now try to adopt when speaking and disciplining our children is to get to their hearts. We help them to see and acknowledge that the reason why they are really struggling to obey us is because they are really struggling to trust us as their parents. In turn, even in a loving family environment, that trust needs to be earned.

Exactly the same applies to our relationship with our perfectly loving heavenly Father. Luther is famously attributed to having penned, 'The sin underneath all our sins is to trust the lie of the serpent that we cannot trust the love and grace of Christ and must take matters into our own hands'. In this chapter I have been pushing for a change in our attitude towards our possessions and time. Of course a holiday from our normal routine is good and necessary. Of course some money is essential. We need to be wise in the use of both our time and our money. But above all we need to exercise our trust in God more. We need to trust him that when we sacrificially invest both these resources in his service, we will be acting in the only sensible way for Christians. It may seem strange at first for many of us to do so. Our Christian culture may even attempt to label us as a bit extreme. But that might actually be the very reaction to confirm we are doing something essential.

2

Careerism:

Reputations and Sandcastles

Work, work, work

I understand the pressures that many individuals are under. The responsibilities you have to meet are far from small. In any given day you only have twenty-four hours in which to accomplish an insurmountable list of things. The non-negotiables are obvious: sleep; eat; wash. That last one has become increasingly complex. While being presentable is of course an admirable desire, there is a real danger, even among Christians, to look perfectly groomed before leaving the house. Then most people work and work and work, for a whole host of reasons.

Individuals differ on their biblical understanding of the purpose of work. Some see every job as a vocation, bringing in the fullness of God's blessing to a sin-soaked world. Work is such an integral part of our identity and what it means to be made in God's image, and gives us dignity, value and worth. Working for the good of others (using the natural resources of the earth to benefit everyone) is itself a proclamation of our sure and certain hope of the new heavens and earth where we will experience the fullness of God's perfect material creation forever. Alternatively, others point out that, especially in the New Testament, very little store is laid upon the 'calling' of work itself. We largely work only to feed our faces and have enough to share with others. Therefore work is not so much an activity of the kingdom as simply a part of this life. We need to work in order to fuel our bodies and have money to finance the verbal proclamation of the gospel.

Regardless of our own viewpoint, our beliefs about the final judgment have a significant impact on the place and value we give to our work in the present. One day this world and our work in it is going to come to an end. Whether or not we think our jobs will have a direct correlation in the world to come, and therefore whether eternity gives an extra dimension of value to our work, is not my concern here. My point is that we often get so entirely wrapped up in our jobs, or they consume all our time and energy, that we never have a chance to think about them from any theological point of view. For most of us, all we can think about are the mortgages we have to pay, the cars we must maintain, the hobbies or holidays that need financing, the weddings to save for, the school uniforms to buy and the pensions to pay into.

However, while the normal demands of life require a steady source of income, I suspect for many people there is something else that drives them: their work goes hand in hand with their reputation. This is a real problem. Work, like money, has the annoying habit of affecting something deep, and sometimes dark, within our own hearts. We can convince ourselves that we are working really, really hard to meet all our responsibilities. In actual fact we are working to prove ourselves, to justify our existence and to persuade ourselves that we really do matter.

As an aside it may surprise many to learn that this is just as much a problem among those who are in ministry as it is in the rest of the working world. While a pastor or minister may be working very hard to be humble, he might be taking great pride in the accolades that people heap on him for his pseudo-humility. While he might be seeking to promote the name of Jesus, his heart could be longing for people to make much of his own name too. While he might know that he should pay no attention to the size of his friend's growing church, he might secretly be dying inside from the intransigence of his own congregation. This explains so much of the depression, division, disappointment and drop-outs in ministry. At the root of all this, as in any job, our hearts long for recognition, and this has the potential to wreck any ministry.

I do understand something of the huge obligations associated with work. At the same time we are so busy pouring ourselves out for the sake of our responsibilities and reputations that we fail to see the danger we are in. Our true need – to define ourselves in terms of our relationship with our Maker – gradually diminishes and dies. We can sacrifice ourselves and our families on the altar of work without even knowing it … simply because we are so busy.

Focus now … on the not yet

Jesus of course spoke on many occasions about this very problem. We focus on the things that appear on our immediate horizon, but he wants us to look well beyond that. It is my own personal but deepening conviction that when preachers apply the truth of God's word to our lives today, far too little is said concerning the immense and imminent tide of eternity that is about to break over this world. On that day much of what we have spent our lives labouring for will simply be washed away, like the sandcastles children build below the tide line on the beach. Regardless of how much effort they spend on trying to keep the encroaching tide from touching their creations, the tide cannot be stopped. And despite every defence built, the castle simply crumples.

Much of the contemporary emphasis in preaching and church life in general is in danger of being fatally imbalanced. The focus is almost exclusively on the immediate relevance and applications for people's lives in the here and now. Our attention would be more profitably directed if we fixed it on the eternal significance of God's actions and promises (though for most people this seems like the far-distant future). Then the practical applications would arise more naturally from our own hearts and therefore have far more of a life-changing impact.

In Luke 14 Jesus tells a story about a party. As he is speaking in the presence of the Pharisees, he has a very unfriendly crowd. However, Jesus' purpose is to confront these incredibly religious and yet tragically cold-hearted leaders. He wants them to see their true standing in relation to God's kingdom.

In the story a leading light in the local community decides to throw something of a party. He invites all his family, friends and colleagues. The invitation had been extended many months before. Initially, it most likely received a very warm welcome, with everyone responding that they had saved the date. Then on the very day of party the excuses start coming in.

One has a new plot of real estate where he plans to put a state-of-the-art tennis court. He is sorry to have to cancel. The other has seriously increased his horse power – or ox power at any rate – and wants to go for a test drive. Yet another has just got himself involved in the greatest, most costly, yet deeply rewarding partnership of his life: a wife.

There is nothing wrong with any of these things, in and of themselves. In fact, in other parts of the Bible they are all seen as great gifts from God. Here, however, they are used as excuses – as distractions – as things that divert the people's focus from their first and original intention.

Obviously these people were initially on speaking terms with their host, otherwise they would not have received an invitation. But now they no longer value that relationship. I'm sure we have all done the same. We've said, 'Yes,' to some invitation, but then when a better offer has come our way, we have scraped around to find some convenient excuse to break our original commitment. This is where the problem really lies. It is not simply that we have failed to follow through on our commitment, but that such flakiness doesn't value our relationship with our host. While our life may be busy, with many obligations and calls on our time, Jesus makes clear the greatest demand on our attention should be living in the light of this certain future date. In making ourselves ready to be there, as we have promised, we are already saying something about the value of our relationship with the host. At this point it is important to remember who Jesus is speaking to in this parable: the Pharisees. They, above all people, ought to have been eagerly anticipating the beginning of the party. Their long-awaited Messiah had appeared. Jesus guaranteed that when the party begins in earnest, entrance will not be refused to all who trust him. But the Pharisees have become distracted by many other 'religious' and self-justifying pursuits. They have lost their focus. In the end they actually miss the party.

Working to get eternity into our hearts

We live in the time between Jesus' first coming and his promised return, when the true party – the party to end all parties – will begin. The question is, will we be ready? As we live in the light of that great day, we too need to be careful not to forget him and the relationship we have with the Father through him. The warning seems plain: if we break our relationship with Jesus – even if we simply begin to take it for granted or treat the invitation we've accepted as the same as any other occasion – that action is fatal.

As much as we want to say that this is not true of us, the facts are difficult to ignore. Many of us sacrifice hours in pursuing our careers, at the expense of getting ready for the ultimate party. We can spend enormous amounts of our hard-earned cash on our next holiday, the latest piece of tech or our well-furnished pension pot. We fail to see all these are temporal and passing away. We even pass these priorities unthinkingly on to our children. We may convince ourselves that the best course of action is to send them to the school that churns out the highest achievers. We do this not realising that the school's entire ethos burns a love for the world into their hearts that ensures they will never prize heaven. Then we reach the end of our days, which we have filled with the things of this world, and find we feel no desire ourselves to enter fully into the joy that is every Christian's inheritance in Christ Jesus.

Our problem is that we often treat our relationship with the Lord of heaven and earth as a means to an end, for example to increase our earthly pleasure. Anything that gets in the way of this is too much of an inconvenience. We need a healthy dose of eternal reality to fix our sights on the endless expanse of future glory. Jesus knew the best was yet to come, so died to secure it for us, having endured the hardship, disdain and rejection of this world. In him it is already ours! No amount of work, or recognition or worldly security will ever come close to the infinite joy that is being kept for us. Yet our gaze is woefully short-sighted.

This affects our priorities towards others too. Many of us find spending quality time with our families is too costly because it doesn't fit with our programme for self-improvement. Opening the Bible with our children is hard enough after a busy day, but it is impossible if we have not already spiritually fed ourselves and wooed our own hearts away from the siren calls of this world. If we can't meet these basic responsibilities in our homes, then giving anything, even our prayers, for the building up of our local church family is out of the question. We might turn up on a Sunday morning, but for many that is about all we do because we are so spent and distracted. We are utterly oblivious to the burning hot purity of the God we say we worship. Instead we just sit there comatosed by the world. Coming to church ready to attribute to God his proper worth, to reorientate our hearts to find their satisfaction in knowing Jesus and to encourage others that they are right to live for God is nowhere on our radar.

The parable ends with a strong warning. Jesus effectively says, 'Look, you can be sure of this … heaven will be full' (Luke 14:23)! While this sounds like great news, it will be full only with those who prize their invitation over and above anything else they have in this life. It will only be full of those whose focus is on being there. In the parable the master is angry at those who spurn his party and sends out new invitations to others.

It is the poor and needy who will actually enjoy that heavenly banquet. In other words, it will be those who do not live for this world because they have very little in it to live for. In Jesus' day the 'poor, the crippled, the blind and the lame' (Luke 14:21) would have been thrown to the margins of society.

Jesus is not simply championing the cause of the oppressed here; his point is more theological. He is talking to the religious adherents, who take pride in their performance. They justify themselves by their work, have a sense of superiority because of what they do and feel very much at the centre of action in this world. Yet these very respectable, religious people are in great danger of being shut out of the heavenly party forever. The stories of God's long-suffering patience, spilling over in his furious wrath with his chosen people because of their casual worship, are replete in the Old Testament. Take heed: hell won't be filled just with the Hitlers of this world; hell will be populated with the unsuspecting: the homeowners, the hard workers, the serial holiday makers and the respectable, decent people who have simply lost their focus.

Jesus was the most loving man who ever lived and yet he drew a line – a very definite line – in the sand. This line, unlike the sandcastles we build, is not washed away by the tide of time. In fact this line is what divides everyone for eternity. On one side are those who are still building their lives on the shifting and shaky foundations of this world. These are people who want to leave a mark on this world, but make no preparation for the world to come. On the other side are those who have come to their senses and can see that there is only one city whose foundations cannot be moved because its designer and builder is God himself (Heb. 11:10).

The right reputation
I am not advocating that you run to the other extreme, embracing the life of a drop-out. My goal is more nuanced

than that. Whatever your station in life, challenge the accepted norms of your particular culture. Society needs Christians everywhere. Some need to be in high society while others must be comfortable on a council estate. Some need to not be intimidated by investment bankers while others must be unafraid of betting shops and building sites. The important thing in all these places is that you are confident and comfortable to be a Christian. Your peers ought to see you as someone with an extra dimension to your life.

Christians will also be concerned for the things that this world does not value. As life is increasingly devalued in Western society, Christians will advocate for the preciousness of all life. As families break down and traditional marriage disintegrates, Christians will speak out for God-honouring patterns in culture. But Christians will work hardest to alleviate eternal suffering by proclaiming and sharing the gospel. To the world this is folly; the message of the cross is one of weakness and stupidity. But to those who are being saved, it is the very power and wisdom of God (1 Cor. 1:18–25).

At some point, whatever world we inhabit, it should think you have missed out on the very best it has to offer – according to its own standards. As a Christian you very well might! But if this is because you have kept a tight hold on Jesus' invitation and are organising your life to be at his party, then in the end you will not be the one who suffers disappointment.

Value your relationship with your maker. This is what will really last and really matter in the end.

An unlikely pairing

One Friday night, my wife and I were watching *The Graham Norton Show*. Matt Damon was on the famous red sofa and the conversation turned to the occasion when Damon won an Oscar for Best Actor at twenty-seven for *Good Will Hunting*. The interview was made all the more poignant because Robin Williams, his co-star, had recently committed suicide. I would not be surprised if Williams' tragic death had not caused Damon to revisit that night with visceral emotion.

Damon said that as he sat looking at his little golden statue, he had something of an epiphany: 'Imagine chasing that and not getting it, and getting it finally in your eighties or your nineties with all of life behind you and realising what an unbelievable waste ...' Graham Norton was transfixed, as probably the entire viewing audience was. I certainly was drawn in. Damon had assumed something of a philosophical air, having achieved significant success when still relatively young. As he uttered those words 'unbelievable waste', he fixed Norton in his gaze. Such a view is rarely heard anywhere, never mind from Hollywood, the Mecca of celebrity stardom. He swept aside the delusion of countless hundreds if not thousands of people with those two simple words, which many must have found devastating.

Damon himself was almost struggling to articulate his thoughts at this point: 'Because it can't ...' he said. 'Do you know what I mean?'

Norton, who is normally good at keeping the conversation going, seemed himself to be slightly at sea. In response to Damon's question, he blurted out, 'It can't be good enough!' At which point Damon jumped on this and proclaimed, 'Right ... it can't fill you up. If that's a hole that you have, that won't fill it.'

Lifting his eyes heavenward, Damon declared, 'I felt so, like, *blessed* to have that awareness at twenty seven.'

Then, as if that was not enough of a moral lesson for one Friday night, he crowned it all by saying: 'My heart broke for a second, it's like I imagined another one of me, an old man, kind of saying, "Oh my, where did my life go ... what have I done ... and then it is over."' Having our eyes focused on what is truly going to last and will satisfy deep down now is crucial. Matt Damon and Jesus Christ are a most unlikely pairing, but we all need to listen to this insight. The gospel is that if we are putting our trust in Jesus Christ, he has deposited into our spiritual bank account eternal riches that will 'never perish, spoil or fade' (1 Pet. 1:4). And again, 'For you know the grace of our Lord Jesus Christ, that though he was rich, yet for your sake he became poor, so that you through his poverty might become rich' (2 Cor. 8:9). That is the simple and yet stunning message of the cross. No amount of work, no success in any career, no worldly accolade at the end of the day will ever come anywhere close to competing with all that Jesus is and has in store for us. As the popular quote goes, 'No one ever said on their death bed, "I wish I had spent more time at the office."'

My prayer is that this understanding will redirect many from being fatally short-sighted. Your time and money spent building your family up in godliness will not go wasted. Your time and money spent building up your church family in godliness will not go wasted. Join me in doing something for the eternal kingdom of Jesus Christ. Then in a mere twenty or thirty years or so (if God should allow that), when your life really is all over, the true party can begin!

3

Sentimentalism:
Old Age, Old Adage, Old Advantage

Message on a bottle

In the most recent retelling of Winston Churchill's life story, the film *Darkest Hour*, Gary Oldman asks a very contemporary question. The scene begins with Oldman portraying Churchill as uncertain how to approach the prospect of meeting King George VI to form a new wartime government. Churchill's wife, Clementine, played by Kristin Scott Thomas, reassuringly encourages him to simply be himself. The camera pulls back to reveal Churchill standing in front of an entire wall, decked with a vast array of hats. He procrastinates with his characteristic guttural grumble. Then, still staring at the hats, he candidly responds, 'Yes, but which self shall I be?' If we can allow for the poetic licence of the silver screen, it appears that the question of identity is nothing new. Over two hundred years ago, John Newton is reputed to have quipped, 'I am a riddle to myself.' However, there does seem to be something of a deepening identity crisis today.

Different

More and more people are finding different ways, both online and – increasingly – in reality, to express multiple and sometimes even contradictory sides to their own personhood. The famous alcoholic drink Smirnoff has run a campaign with the slogan 'Labels are for bottles not people'. The message is clear: you are free to be whoever you want to be. It seems strange to be writing this, but the mantra that says simply 'Be true to yourself' is quickly going out of fashion. While that was the dominant note of the early years of the new millennium, we are now in uncharted territory. How can anyone actually be true to themselves when in fact the self in question is now so multifaceted that there is no concrete centre to which one can be true to?

There is yet another surprising feature to this increasing social and personal fragmentation. You might expect such discussions around the 'decentring' of identity among those still emerging from the latter years of teenage angst. What I did not expect to find, however, was this problem appearing in the older generations too – those in the latter years of their careers, who are competent in their jobs and who even hold senior positions. If you were to visit them in their office, their surgery or their studio, you would find them reassuringly knowledgeable about their subjects. Afterwards, if you were then to take a quick look at their Facebook posts or other social media platforms, you might think that they were two completely different people.

Take any of the hot topics around today, like transgenderism, abortion or same-sex marriage, and you can find contradictory opinions being expressed by the same person, depending on the context in which they find themselves. Perhaps such inner conflicts have always existed, but I'm not sure that is what Gary Oldman's Churchill meant when deciding which self he ought to be. No doubt Churchill had some very fixed views about the cultural trends of his day. Yet today we have the opportunity to be fluid and experiment with completely different views because we can appear in so many disconnected arenas. Not only does the youthful sub-culture try to assert itself against the prevailing way of seeing the world, but shockingly such confusion exists today in the more seasoned generation too, as they have also seized the opportunities afforded by being online. Are we all becoming less certain about what we actually think concerning the ever evolving narratives that weave together to produce our culture? The last twist is that this increasing personal fragmentation of the senior citizens in society is just as much a problem within the church.

Within the church, turf wars are of course nothing new, but the concerns within the different factions are. Divisions are no longer over the upkeep of buildings and which families have tenure over particular pews. They are now marked by incredibly emotive opinions on whatever the latest controversial issue in wider society happens to be. The deeply troubling thing is that no one can any longer assume simply because someone can say the Nicene Creed by rote (a dying art of an older generation) that they will hold the line on any ethical or moral question of the day. So, for example, an older individual might give the impression they are in agreement with the counter-cultural stance of his or her church on any given Sunday, but that very same afternoon they might 'like' a Facebook post that flatly contradicts such assent.

This makes leading a church incredibly difficult. In a sense it is wrong to suggest a significant realignment of loyalties is taking place because that implies they still are definable. Today the old, familiar lines of division are so porous that it is nearly impossible to predict anything that will come out of an individual's mouth. A mature woman might be a dyed-in-the wool Anglican who loves the traditional form of morning worship, and yet online be as progressive as her teenage grandchildren on matters of sexual morality.

The focus of this chapter, therefore, is to plead with the older generation to stand firm to gospel truth. The watching world needs to see that you actually believe in something and live for such a belief. Younger generations of Christians need to see too that you might be prepared even to die, if not at least suffer some loss, for such a belief.

Pulling rank

There is a clear biblical reason for my appeal. As far as I can see, when people of senior years speak, it is prudent for younger people to listen. If the Bible was an airline company, then it would unashamedly reserve most of its priority seating for those of a certain vintage and above. The younger ones on board would also be expected for the most part to comply with the well-worn adage that young people should 'be seen and not heard'. Of course, there are bad impositions of such hierarchy. My father-in-law often tells my children that when he was a little boy 'being seen and not heard' meant that he wasn't even able to sit at the same table as adults when they were eating. That was 'being not seen or heard'. However, time and again throughout the Bible, and of course in many more traditional societies still today, older people are due the respect of their years.

Moses, for example, can be seen following the advice of his pagan father-in-law, Jethro. While Jethro may not have held the same doctrine as Moses, this did not stop Moses from recognising wisdom when he saw it. Then, in due course, the mantle fell to Moses himself. As an older man, he came to instruct a whole new generation of Israelites since their stubborn forefathers had all died in the desert for refusing to obey God. The entire book of Proverbs is an extended example of this: 'My son, do not forget my teaching, but keep my commands in your heart, for they will prolong your life many years and bring you peace and prosperity' (Prov. 3:1–2). In the Bible we see many occasions where neglecting the wisdom of those more advanced in years caused a problem, to put it mildly. One example is Rehoboam, who abandoned the counsel of the old, instead following the advice of the young (2 Chr. 10:8). Such folly, which led to the rebellion of the ten northern tribes of Israel, split the kingdom into two.

I know God does not always chose those of an older age to fulfil his purposes. Samuel was called by the Lord as a boy. God tells Jeremiah, 'before you were born I set you apart' (Jer. 1:5). Indeed, when the world expects the eldest and the strongest, who they presume is the wisest, to be used by God, very often God delights in subverting this. Joseph and David were the youngest of all their brothers. We see the same scenario with Esau and Jacob, and with Ishmael and Isaac. The elder brother in Jesus' parable of the prodigal son receives substantial criticism.

God often does take our preconceptions and turns them on their head, simply to show that he is in charge and it is on him we should depend. We see this too when he uses those the world deems weak, forgotten and powerless to accomplish his plans. Of course, there is no guarantee that the older you get, the wiser or more sanctified you become. Sometimes it is the older generation who go off the rails and require an intervention of God to keep things on track. Nevertheless, the general principle is that age carries a certain weight that the younger members of the family ignore to their peril.

A whole new world?

Some might think that this value on older age changes with Jesus' birth into our world. The Pharisees felt the full force of Jesus' divine rancour when trying to put him in his place as a younger – as well as more popular and, in their eyes, increasingly troublesome – rabbi. They wanted to assert their senior religious position, insisting their older age outranked him. However, they were of course overlooking one important fact: Jesus is able to say 'before Abraham was born, I am' (John 8:58). This was no momentary lapse in grammar on Jesus' part, but an assertion of deity that outranked the Pharisees' claim to authority on every level. It was the ultimate put-down to those who looked 'older' than himself and who had been in their job longer than he had been on earth.

Yet presumably Jesus would have shown due deference to those who, in earthly terms, were older than him. While we know relatively little about his family life as a child, Jesus said that he came to fulfil the law (Matt. 5:17), which included honouring his earthly parents (Matt. 19:17–19). Should we have had the pleasure of sitting in on one of his family meals, we would have been able to say that Joseph and Mary's son never once was ill-behaved, bad mannered or used the wrong tone! Of course Jesus repeatedly challenged putting family ties above kingdom priorities (Mark 3:31–35; Luke 9:57–62). This, though, would never have led him to treat his family with contempt.

God has built the world in a way where age does matter, since it brings with it a certain wisdom – the advantage of hindsight perhaps. Excepting Jesus himself, we rarely find a young boy or girl who possesses a wisdom beyond their years and at the same time the humility that ensures this doesn't make them proud. Perhaps Josiah came close, but he is the rarest of exceptions (2 Kgs. 23:25). My point, however, in contrast to this biblical trend and indeed expectation, is that today many of the older, senior and therefore supposedly wiser and godlier people sitting in our pews are just as much at sea as the younger people they are beside.

We find this same teaching that older people in a home set-up or church family ought to be respected by their juniors in the rest of the New Testament. What are referred to as the Household Codes (technically, the *Haustafeln*!) in the letters of Paul and Peter are perhaps some of the most contentious and explosive passages that any preacher dare venture into today. Take, for example, Ephesians 6:1–4:

> *Children, obey your parents in the Lord, for this is right.*
> *'Honour your father and mother' – which is the first*
> *commandment with a promise – 'so that it may go well with*
> *you and that you may enjoy long life on the earth.'*

> *Fathers, do not exasperate your children; instead, bring them*
> *up in the training and instruction of the Lord.*

Not so long ago, such commands would have been met with a prolonged collective yawn and bored disdain. Today, however, such teaching might induce a city-wide riot. If you try telling children that they should actually do as they are told, that they are not in control of the family diary or that they should even be disciplined, you might be in danger of suffering not only the looks of confusion among your congregation but the condemnation of the courts.

If we rewind to the close of the previous chapter in Ephesians 5:22–33, we find ourselves in even hotter water with the instruction on men's and women's roles in a marriage. Any pastor brave enough to tell his congregation that wives should submit to their husbands today is lighting the proverbial touch paper that could potentially explode his church. Such teaching is often completely silenced today because our particular culture is consumed (sometimes rightly) with the (sometimes appalling) treatment that women have had to suffer at the hands of bullying men.

However, it is worth understanding that when Paul originally wrote this letter, the call for men to sacrifice themselves for their wives would have caused a similar volcanic eruption among the men in society. By and large, any self-respecting male would never have considered serving others, never mind any women. Yet this was no deterrent to Paul, who clearly saw the implications of what it means to live under the perfect and eternal reign of Jesus Christ. Husbands are to be living examples of Jesus' sacrificial love for the church, as they willingly, joyfully and daily lay down their lives for their wives. In the same way, wives submitting to their husbands is a biblical truth, regardless of its reception in any society.

The different New Testament authors were confronted by varying cultural assumptions, but it is noticeable that they did not necessarily seek to overthrow each culture immediately. Much needed confronting and condemning, but some of the universal social patterns were treated more carefully. This is seen in the classic example of slavery by the particular approach that Paul takes when addressing Philemon. Essentially Philemon is instructed by Paul to accept back his runaway slave, Onesimus, either without any penalty or by passing any penalty to Paul to bear (Phil. 10, 15–19). Not only, therefore, does Paul show how a substitutionary understanding of the cross effects his relationship with other Christians, but he uses this to urge Philemon to set aside normal cultural practices meted out to disobedient slaves.

Membership in God's family is the new paradigm by which all other relationships are now to be recalibrated. This transcends every other cultural barrier. These relationships are, after all, the most enduring of all because they are built upon Jesus' resurrection from the dead.

Most modern people are troubled that Paul does not stand up and blatantly challenge slavery. Their objection, though, is often crude in that they equate the slavery of the Bible with the grotesque practices of the modern slave industry. They fail to see that for many in biblical times slavery was in fact a chosen career path, and for good reason as it often provided security and safety it. They also fail to see that Paul's letter expresses brotherhood and sisterhood in Christ, which would eventually erode any abuses and in time the very endorsement of slavery itself.

In the light of the cross and resurrection, every expression of hierarchy is not necessarily obliterated but exists under the regulating instruction of the Bible. The lines of authority continue for the good of all. Workers still have bosses. Children still have parents. Wives still have husbands. And the young still have their seniors.

Mission of the mature

I earlier stated that many of the older, senior and therefore supposedly wiser and godlier people sitting in our pews are just as much at sea as the younger people in terms of their biblical understanding. Yet we have seen that the Bible urges older people to have considerable influence over those younger than them, especially in matters of the faith. That is the challenge.

Here is what Paul urges in Titus 2:1–6:

You, however, must teach what is appropriate to sound doctrine. Teach the older men to be temperate, worthy of respect, self-controlled, and sound in faith, in love, and in endurance.

Likewise, teach the older women to be reverent in the way they live, not to be slanderers or addicted to much wine, but to teach what is good. Then they can urge the younger women to love their husbands and children, to be self-controlled and pure, to be busy at home, to be kind, and to be subject to their husbands, so that no one will malign the word of God.

Similarly, encourage the young men to be self-controlled.

In this one short passage Paul covers almost everything we have just been talking about. Paul does not see our new status in Christ as completely negating every or even any difference between us. We are indeed all one in Christ, in terms of our sin and our need of him as our eternal Saviour. But, once saved and new creations, we are to inhabit the old structures still as men and women, as husbands and wives, as young and old. In these roles we are each called to assume our appropriate responsibilities as Christians 'so that no one will malign the word of God' (v. 5).

Paul particularly has plenty to say to older people. Among the many character traits these older people are to display and exemplify are the qualities of steadiness and self-control. Their particular cultural context was that of the infamous Cretans, who according to one of their own prophets were 'always liars, evil beasts, lazy gluttons' (Tit. 1:12). Not exactly the holiday image you would want to be promoting abroad! The Cretan Christians might have easily excused themselves as having been steeped in their old ways for far too long. Or, if they changed their lifestyle, no doubt they would have been a source of ridicule, or at least a conversational point, down at their local watering hole. In the midst of such personal temptation and social pressure, they could easily have capitulated and followed their old ways, conforming once again to what they knew best. Paul's concern is for the younger men and women who start following Christ – from whom would they take their lead? Titus, though presumably not the oldest in the congregation, is to model submission to God's word by teaching what accords with sound doctrine. In response, the different groups are to hold on to such teaching and put it into practice. They are ruled now by a different authority – no longer of the world, but of the word.

After a few years of visiting the very elderly in their homes, I often left thinking that old age can be relatively enjoyable. Of course, this is as long as you have a certain level of good health and support. Old age has certain advantages, of which I thought the most enviable was the right to say whatever you like. There comes a stage in life when you simply give up caring what other people think! I often found myself thinking, 'Well, they've earned that entitlement.' But in the light of this passage, I think I must stand corrected. Old age is not an occasion simply to let rip with your particular sinful proclivities. Old age is yet another opportunity to practise godliness that will shape and train up a whole new generation.

It is my experience that the greatest need among younger generations such as mine is to find older people who are prepared to be courageous enough to remain sober-minded and steadfast in the face of massive cultural shifts. These two qualities are at a premium today because as the older generation looks to their progeny, they feel a huge emotional investment. What loving father or mother does not want to embrace their children in all that they are and choose to do? What devoted grandparent does not want to see their little grandchildren affirmed and encouraged in their loves and passions? But the trouble today is that so much of what the younger generation wants to be applauded for is simply madness. We experiment with absolutely everything, and it is tearing our society and indeed our very selves apart. Jobs are temporary, marriages are expendable, sexuality is fluid and personhood is a guessing game. The last thing we need is to be affirmed in these patterns.

As a father of four young children, I realise that my children are not yet at the stage of challenging the boundaries my wife and I have set as Christian parents. We have not yet reached the point where our worries keep us awake at night. No doubt that time will come. What I have noticed, however, among many parents who are a little further down the track and even among the grandparents of young teenagers and adults, is their complete lack of steadfastness on issues that are central to a God-honouring view of the world.

Older Christian men and women, you now have a new mission field before you. Older men, your mission is to be 'temperate, worthy of respect, self-controlled, and sound in faith, in love, and in endurance' (Tit. 2:2). How great are the temptations that confront you! How much the younger men need to see you do battle with your sin. The temptations to be carefree, rude, profligate, open-minded, selfish and sentimental are constant. For older women the temptations are no less. They are 'to be reverent in the way they live, not to be slanderers or addicted to much wine, but to teach what is good' (v. 3). It appears the sins of the tongue, and its tastes, are particularly dangerous for you. The younger women need to witness you fighting these sins, along with the other temptations they face of not loving their husband or children, or of being lazy and rebellious in their home (Tit. 2:5).

Likewise, take the time to be truly loving and talk to younger Christians about the decisions they are making and the reason they are living as they do. Talk sense when it is needed. Hold on to the truth. That is the most loving, supportive and encouraging thing you can do.

If, in contrast, you are a young man, find yourself a godly older man who can model Christ-likeness. If you are a young woman, find a godly older woman who can do the same. Be open about who that might be, search carefully and pray that God would put just this sort of person in your life. It might just be the making of you.

Imagine a gospel-shaped community where everyone is playing their part: men and women, rich and poor, old and young. Imagine a place where everyone is so sure of their value and worth because they are confident in God's everlasting love for them. Imagine the richness of such relationships and the joy of such belief. It would be a place where people of all ages and from all backgrounds could shelter from the storms of a confused and confusing culture. It would be a place where the particular sinful problems of each group could be dealt with in a challenging and yet compassionate way. The gospel is and will forever remain the power of God for the salvation and ongoing transformation of all, regardless of our age.

4

Nationalism:
Borders and Belief

Shaken and stirred

Hate crimes seem to be just beneath the surface in Northern
Ireland, my home country. There is no spoiler alert needed
here: as most of the world knows, we have a long and infamous
past of not getting along with one another. Little more than
thirty years ago, if you should had been out for a drive and
happen to find yourself in a community where the majority of
people didn't share your personal political, religious or cultural
heritage, you would have been wise to find the quickest way
out. Actually, if you didn't have the same local accent or
'pronunciation', then James Bond's revolving licence plate,
along with his bullet-proof glass and maybe even his legendary
ejecting seat, would have served you well. Without delving too
deeply into the intricacies of all this, it is worrying. Northern
Ireland has, despite a relatively small population, a staggering
number of churches per capita, and yet the level of violence
committed in the name of religion, and specifically in the name
of Christianity, is sickening. For this reason my father forbade

conversation about religion, along with politics, at our dinner time. Having grown up in Northern Ireland all his life, religion – as far as he could see – was the primary cause for so many of the deaths he read about in his newspaper. He therefore reasoned simply that he did not want such arguments while enjoying his daily consumption of potatoes. (The fact he has a son who now works in the church is one of those strange little twists of God's irony.)

It is a very painful fact that for all its Christian heritage and churches, Northern Ireland was a deeply divided community and for many a dangerous place to live. While things have 'improved' ... slightly, as I write this our own Northern Irish politicians are not talking with one another and so we have had to ask the government in Westminster to take over leading our local affairs again. Furthermore, the news reports still talk about hate crimes. However, these crimes are now committed mostly against those who have made the brave decision to leave their own country of origin and to try to make a home for themselves here. Such xenophobia either bubbles up in violence – showing that beneath the surface we haven't changed at all – or results in doors being kept firmly closed because we simply don't want to accommodate 'others'.

I saw the same shocking xenophobia in the Republic of Ireland. In 2004 I had started working for an Anglican church-planting agency in Dublin city centre. I was conducting a survey to ascertain what the local shop owners and residents thought were some of their community's greatest problems. Perhaps our church could meet them. The number one problem the local Irish people cited was all the 'foreigners' flooding into their city and country. You can imagine the sickening feeling I had in the pit of my stomach as I took these findings back to my church that had grown precisely because of this 'problem'. The fact that this church of internationals is still there and attempting to reach out to such a community of xenophobes is testimony to the greatness of God's generosity.

This worrying drift towards the darker side of nationalism is not limited to certain communities within Northern Ireland or indeed Ireland as an island. The free movement of people worldwide has been accompanied by this phenomenon of intolerance, with which every country is currently struggling to cope. In Ireland it may express itself primarily in terms of nationalism. However, the world watches in some disbelief as headlines continue to emerge from the USA concerning primarily the colour of your skin. In the UK, Brexit is a massive concern, but the huge discrepancies between the classes and the north/south divide remain unresolved. Then across Europe as a whole it is seen as a clash of Islam meeting the post-Christian West. Such inability to welcome those who are different not only characterises the storylines of continents and nations. In cities around the world – as spiritually enlightened global trotters settle into traditional communities, as progressive liberals gentrify sleepy conservative backwaters and as capitalists collide with socialists – the difficulty of living with one another is huge. The world seems to be something of a social cocktail that has been both shaken and stirred, and is certainly not to everyone's liking.

Insipid Christianity

At a grass-root level, this concern over our national identities should matter for every Christian. It matters when the new family moving in next door is from Nigeria and knows nothing of our culture. It matters when suddenly our mono-cultural church finds itself surrounded by a social housing project built to cater for the newest wave of immigrants from the Middle East. It matters when our children are confronted with an ideological agenda in their schools that insists all religions are the same and there is no monopoly on truth today. The kaleidoscopic mixture of politics, religion and culture is everywhere. The question is do we care enough to engage with it for the sake of God's glory and the plight of the lost, or are there other idols that matter more to us than these?

Recently much has been written about the church's mission. It is a long-debated topic that can polarise Christians. My prime concern here is that many Christians are so overrun with the frantic pace of their everyday life that they don't engage in such debates. After they have spent their energy and time in their earthly pursuits, they often cannot bring themselves even to worry about them. Ordinary Christianity, therefore, is rendered so bland and boring that it has little or nothing to say in any debate, full stop. To the wider world such disinterested Christians produce an uninteresting Christianity that is quickly and easily forgotten.

In my context the progress of the mission of the church is, for the most part, in serious decline. Ireland, once famously the land of saints and scholars, now resembles something closer to a spiritual waste land. Churches litter the countryside and cities as a distant reminder of what people used to believe. In Northern Ireland the religious feud has silenced many from speaking out with any winsome conviction. In the Republic of Ireland the majority of people are not interested in listening to the institutional church because its credibility has already been silenced largely by its own deviant abusive actions. This has produced today a real distaste for much serious religious discussion. Along with the prevalent and strong postmodern bent, talking in public about your religious convictions is a rare and uncomfortable experience for most Christians. Despite some rare and commendable exceptions, the majority of ordinary Irish Christians have swallowed the view that their faith is a personal thing and therefore incredibly private.

If we mix these two together, we have an insipid and unattractive gospel that has no depth or dimension to its glory. It is no wonder that many would not find accepting a dinner invitation from such a Christian an appealing option. What have we forgotten?

Self-obsessed Jesus?

The simple answer is Jesus. Yes, the classic Sunday School response! But in seriousness I think we really have forgotten, or perhaps for some never fully discovered, the real stature of the biblical Jesus. He will always be interesting when properly understood. In the Bible's pages lie all that any Christian will ever need to recover a living and vibrant faith.

In Luke's gospel we read about one day when Jesus, recognising the shallowness of his own disciples' relationship with himself, goes on the offensive. It is time for them to take their next step in following him, and that comes in the form of publicly confessing something about him. Jesus, wanting to tackle any misunderstanding, asks his followers who people think he is. They respond, 'Some say John the Baptist, others say Elijah; and still others, that one of the prophets of long ago has come back to life' (Luke 9:19). This is an esteemed group of people to belong to and one that any regular rabbi would have been only too pleased to join – but not Jesus. He is not content to be mentioned in the same league as these spiritual heavyweights, and so he pushes his question further. Looking at his own disciples, he asks them, 'But what about you? Who do you say I am?' (Luke 9:20).

In asking the question this way, Jesus is doing a number of things. Firstly, he is expecting his disciples to have a different opinion of him from the rest of the crowd. Every Christian needs to become quickly comfortable with this reality. The general person's view about the importance and uniqueness of Jesus is going to fall short – far, far short – of the true estimation that any real Christian should have about him. Jesus is using this particular teaching tool to drive a wedge between his followers and the world. It is critical for all Christians to regularly remind ourselves that what we believe about Jesus makes us distinct from everyone else who considers him to be a nice guy, but simply a regular man. Right from the start the mark of the true Christian was that they worshipped Jesus as God — not simply because he had offered one way to understand God. It was revolutionary.

Secondly, Jesus' question highlights that Christianity is a deeply personal belief too. He is interested in what *you* think about him. In other words, he will not accept a proxy faith or any argument that suggests simply that you must be considered a Christian because your great-grandfather attended a certain church. Living faith in this Jesus is not something that is transmitted genetically, inherited eventually or bestowed institutionally. Living faith in this Jesus is a matter for each individual to make personally, sincerely and willingly for themselves: 'Who do you say that I am?'

The personal dimension to the Christian faith does not however relegate it to the private vaults of our lives. This is the third thing that Jesus is pointing out as he stands before his disciples. Indeed, it is perhaps one of the most valuable lessons that any one of us can learn and relearn today. Personal belief must result in a public response. It should never remain simply and forever more a private faith. The church finds itself in a very compromised position today, and one of its own making. Christians know they ought to be humble and open to all people. The postmodern culture has capitalised on this, taking it a step further to encourage us to say nothing that will offend. Half in agreement, we have sleepwalked into a deafening silence, and we don't know how to wake ourselves up. Or worse still, we'd rather remain in our slumber because then we can enjoy our comfort and not draw attention to ourselves.

The game changer

In Luke's gospel, Peter leads the way for us all to follow, answering, 'God's Messiah' (Luke 9:20). From that moment forward the entire history of the world was changed forever. Peter's public confession of his personal faith is a statement of such enormous significance that it makes the San Andreas Fault look like a hairline crack on the pavement outside your door.

In Peter's response we have the answer to our 2D, black-and-white, nondescript gospel, plus the answer to every politically correct objection that threatens to muzzle the gospel today. We have the supreme reason to cross every political, social, racial, ethnic, religious, cultural barrier that the world puts in our way. We have the ultimate anathema to all our inane, lazy and unacceptable excuses to reaching out, beyond our comfort zones, to bring the good news of the gospel and all its blessing to others. In effect Peter says to Jesus, 'At last, you've come, and now the story of the world will be completely different'.

Different

The title 'God's Messiah' or 'the Christ' is a technical term. 'Christ' is not Jesus' surname – and simply one among many billions of other names – but the Bible's title reserved for God's unique ruler. It originates right back to Genesis 3 when, in the midst of rightful judgment on Adam's and Eve's sinful rebellion against him, God mercifully promised one who would eventually appear to deal with his universal curse. This promise then begins to pulsate throughout the entire Bible and is deepened and textured over many, many centuries.

It comes to include quintessential passages like Psalm 2 that speak of God's ruler – his Messiah, the Christ and King – dashing to pieces the nations who oppose him, and welcoming all who wisely bow the knee before him. It encompasses Daniel 7, which speaks of the Messiah's kingdom as one that will never pass away. Isaiah adds that this long-promised King is the deliverer who will not only bring back God's people from the four corners of the world, but also cast off the universal darkness that kills: 'It is too small a thing for you to be my servant to restore the tribes of Jacob and bring back those of Israel I have kept. I will also make you a light for the Gentiles, that my salvation may reach to the ends of the earth' (Is. 49:6). In Isaiah this kingly figure also, curiously, merges with that of a suffering servant, who rescues by giving himself to bear the punishment we all deserve (Is. 53:4–12).

When Jesus begins his earthly ministry, this title has therefore become a complex, compelling and almost combustible term. Peter would have understood it in part, but not yet grasped its full scope. Discipleship is often just like that, where we 'see only a reflection as in a mirror' and only 'know in part' (1 Cor. 13:12). We, however, have the benefit of his hindsight. In the light of such a game changer, it would be wise if we were to ask ourselves some serious questions. For example, the first and most crucial question is do we in fact believe this? There is no point troubling ourselves with any other questions if we are as yet still unsure. Do you believe Jesus is God's unique and only Son, who is in a league all by himself? Do you believe that he alone is perfect in every way and never sinned once throughout his life? Do you believe that he is the only way to have peace and an eternal relationship with God because he gave his life on the cross for you? These are the fundamental beliefs of Christianity, and if we truly believe them, we will know how magnificent they are.

If you believe in such a Jesus, please consider the following question: what excuse then do you really have to remain silent about your faith? You may find it uncomfortable to speak about him. I get that – to some extent. But as it is true, and we are those who confess it to be so, we should at least be attempting to share it with others. The salvation Jesus achieved by dying and rising to life again is not for a few select individuals, one particular tribe or even a single nation, but everyone throughout the whole world. The whole Old Testament points to such a multinational, worldwide act of redemption. Not even the gates of hell are able to stand against Jesus. He has laid siege to the fortress of death itself and crushed it. This is what it means for him to be God's Messiah, the long-awaited Christ. It might be argued that what happens next in Luke 9 is the real shock in the passage and our most compelling reason to speak. After Jesus' razor-sharp question and Peter's great revelation, it seems staggering that Jesus says nothing in acknowledgment. Peter's confession is met with Jesus' complete silence. He neither bats an eyelid nor rushes to refuse such a designation. His silence is in fact his deafening confirmation that Peter is absolutely right in what he has just declared. Jesus knows he is on a mission to overthrow the worldwide reign of death, so he simply accepts the title and moves on without further comment. It is surely the clearest, sharpest and brightest green light that any of us need to ascribe greatness to Jesus publicly, just as Peter did.

In fact it gets even better still. Jesus immediately promises that such a confession will be seen to be absolutely true by what he is about to do: rise from the dead. This unprecedented event adds extra incentive for us to open our mouths to speak about Jesus. Jesus' looming mission in Jerusalem will involve being treated as a regular criminal and suffering crucifixion at the hands of the elders, chief priests and scribes. In some of the gospel accounts Peter, immediately after having confessed Jesus to be the Christ, actually takes him aside to reprimand him for talking about dying (Mark 8:31–32). It is as if Peter has not heard Jesus at all. All Peter can think about is Jesus' ministry ending in failure. Peter, however, is the one who has failed to hear how it properly plays out. The angels in Jesus' empty tomb are quick to remind the witnesses that Jesus had repeatedly told his disciples that his death would not end in defeat (Luke 24:4–7). Jesus, immediately after having unashamedly accepted the title to be God's supreme, unique, divine ruler, is promising to prove it by his resurrection. Yes, he must die – this is part of the plan. However, death is not to be the end for him because he is unlike any human who ever lived.

Jesus forces us to acknowledge the difference between him and everyone else. Peter's public confession is the example that we all should follow. Then Jesus' quiet confirmation of his unique identity and his promise to prove it by rising from the dead, as he did, is further incentive to proclaim to all people that he is God's Messiah.

Looking back on all that occurred in Jesus' ministry, death and resurrection should cause our hearts to burn within us. Yet I know from experience that some Christians say they are not interested in evangelism. I am often pigeonholed as someone who is more interested in mission than actually running a regular church, whatever that might be. Such a statement, I sense, is intended to marginalise me and my like. But the Bible tells us Jesus is the Son of God, who died to forgive his enemies and rose to prove his matchless power to save people from every tribe, language and nation. If we truly understand this Jesus, then we should not only understand that we ought to be speaking about him, but should be actively compelled to do so. The gospel transcends every pathetic excuse that we may offer as to why we remain unmoved about evangelism and silent today.

A few short, sharp shocks

Jesus could foresee that in the light of all he was about to achieve, there would be many who would jump on the proverbial bandwagon. From the very start, his power and patience with people had drawn great crowds. It is true that because of the things he taught, many within the crowd often turned away. At the very end he died with only a few of his disciples around him. But he knew that because of the resurrection power he was about to unleash on the world, many people would once again be drawn to those who had the very words of life.

There would be many pretenders: those who would claim to belong to him, but who would display none of the family traits of those who properly understood his call on their lives. Such serious acts of self-deception require the plainest of speech, which is exactly what Jesus administers next: 'Whoever wants to be my disciple must deny themselves and take up their cross daily and follow me' (Luke 9:23).

Having been taken up to such dizzying heights concerning the unique person of Jesus and the place he occupies in the history of the world, this is a searching statement for his followers. Any serious Bible reader cannot but feel the sharpness of such words and know the depths to which they cut. Jesus shows how his lordship impacts the reality of our everyday lives. Believing in him means that he now holds the number-one spot in our lives. We must deny the natural inclination of all our hearts: to be number one ourselves. He does not belong to us and is not to do our bidding. We belong to him and exist to do his will. Therefore to follow Jesus as our Lord means that we should fully expect to have our share of suffering in this world. We are to put ourselves on the cross by dying to our focus on ourselves, our temptation to sin and the lure of this world. This is the normal Christian experience. In this sense the act of believing is not for the faint-hearted: it means being uncompromising with ourselves. The fact that we are to do so 'daily' again underlines that our faith is not some dim distant event in the past but a present, purifying reality. I would say that five short words summarise the testimony of every Christian who has ever lived: 'Jesus is my master now'.

Jesus certainly knows our hearts better than we know them ourselves. He can see the ever-present dangers that lie within them, and therefore calls us to wake up and get on board with his programme. Of course, we will only ever take up such a challenge when we see him as he really is. Then we will understand there is actually no better option than following him, as inconvenient and uncomfortable as our hard hearts might think this to be.

In order to further tease out the effect of his lordship on our lives, Jesus focuses on some of the exact issues that we have already covered in this book. He says those who want 'to save their life' – here and now – will actually 'lose it' in the long run (Luke 9:24). Materialism cannot deliver you when it matters most. Ikea products may be made for the everyday, but they cannot furnish your eternal destiny. Again, those who may 'gain the whole world', achieving all their earthly ambitions, will in the end 'forfeit their very self' (Luke 9:25). Careerism will only carry you so far, leaving you short when it matters the most. Similarly, on the last day, when you are face to face with your Maker and Judge, he will not accept your going soft in your old age: 'Whoever is ashamed of me and my words, the Son of Man will be ashamed of them' (Luke 9:26). Sentimentalism will put you in such a position before the King of the universe.

Such warnings are uncomfortable to consider as we review our Christian lives, but they remain absolutely necessary. We have an endless capacity towards self-deception. Yet Jesus promises to not accept any false claims to follow him, ultimately removing all such pretenders when he comes again. Luke 9:26 therefore ends in this way: 'Whoever is ashamed of me and my words, the Son of Man will be ashamed of them when he comes in his glory and in the glory of the Father and of the holy angels'. Jesus' words ought to be the cause of some sober reflection. He does not make false promises. He promised to prove his uniqueness by rising from the dead, and he did. He promises to remove all those who treat him as a spiritual spare wheel, and he will do so.

In my experience, the popular belief in God is about as close to what Jesus is talking about here as I am to ever beating Usain Bolt's list of world records. So many consider God a nonpersonal, non-interfering, disinterested, Star-Wars-esque type of power that sends comforting tingles up and down our spine. That is the best that our little human imaginations can stretch to and that our lazy hearts will allow. Such belief permits countless adherents to sit through church services and even be active on church committees without the vaguest notion of the sheer majesty and uncompromising sovereignty of the God who is in fact there. Others have what amounts to only a casual belief. Perhaps some 'religious' experience happened like a hiccup in their past. It has a certain abstract interest to them today. But it is only a very small part of their lives when compared to what really sets them on fire. However, Jesus is not looking for casual belief. He is looking for committed believers who are active in their pursuit of all things that please him, who find themselves compelled by his love for others and who count the things of this world as nothing if only some might be saved. Such faith is fully aware and alive to the fact that God is a very personal, intimately committed, all-controlling, passionately focused lover of our souls. Given this, to not live for him is an act of sheer madness.

Bringing the gospel home

Perhaps you are wondering what all this has to do with your neighbour from a different country? Or how should any of this change the way you see the waves of immigrants appearing on the streets of your city? Do I have any idea of the cost it would involve to reach out to those of a different class, colour or creed? Can I seriously be asking you even to reach out to those who historically have caused so much hurt and pain to your community? If that is your thinking, search your heart and ask is Jesus really Lord of all? In turn what then does your silence say about your true estimation of the significance of Jesus? How could we continue to keep our doors closed to those for whom Jesus died? Take my own cultural context. This chapter began with the literary equivalent to motorway rubbernecking as we drove past some of the more embarrassing examples of xenophobia on the island which I call home. Pride of Northern Ireland has stained the witness of many professing Christians all across this island, and continues to do so. I previously mentioned the massive paradox between the sheer saturation of churches there and yet the sickening levels of violence committed under the Christian banner. This is not the only glaring paradox that exists in Ireland, however. The Republic of Ireland's border with Northern Ireland is a topic of much discussion at present. Ever since the UK voted to leave the European Union, the question as to what to do with the Irish border has produced no little consternation. In the end, though, no matter what sort of border the Brexit negotiations produce, it will never be as solid and as clearly defined as the insurmountable border that already exists in the mind of many Northern Irish Christians towards their nearest neighbour.

It is well documented that the Republic of Ireland is in great spiritual need. The majority of their people are not interested in what the church is saying today, especially as for many its message has been eviscerated by its own actions. Recent figures therefore show that the fastest growing religion in Ireland is those who have 'no religion' at all. In fact, those claiming to be Christians, who hold the Bible to be true and reliable, are less than 1% of the population. Among the English-speaking nations of the world, the Republic of Ireland is one of the least serviced in terms of biblical teaching. Yet Northern Ireland, with its abundance of Christians, sits and for the most part looks idly on. I know it is more complicated than I am suggesting here, but my point is that I haven't heard too many people even begin to question what is wrong with this situation.

I hear of Americans theologically engaging with race. Recently some of their very high-profile Christian leaders have apparently publicly broken down in an expression of repentance over sins of racism in the church. On 20 August 2018 the Gospel Coalition website reported, 'Reformed Theological Seminary chancellor Ligon Duncan fought back tears as he repented of racial blindness … "It has taken more than three decades for God to bring this blindness off my heart," he said'. David Platt, John Piper and Tim Keller are among others who have added to this conversation over recent years. I see similar musings in the UK among Christians addressing the issues of class. Many new church plants are seeking to reach across the class divides. Some church-planting networks like Mez McConnell's 20schemes are deliberately focusing on areas where social deprivation is high. Co-Mission in London is seeking to direct more and more of its resources to supporting small, slow-burning church plants in inner-city council estates. Of course this is not to say that there is much work still needed to address the blind spots of churches in America and Britain. A social revolution like that led by Martin Luther King Jr. or William Wilberforce is unlikely. It might even be unnecessary, as church leaders and grass-root movements in the church do the secret, hidden work of building friendships and relationships with their brothers and sisters of a different skin colour or from a different class of society. The encouraging thing is that at least these conversations have a certain traction already. The world needs to see truly integrated and lovingly concerned church families pouring themselves out for one another regardless of any of their social and cultural divisions.

Back in Ireland many of my fellow country people still need to put nationalism in its place. Regrettably this is a conversation that still needs to begin in many quarters of the church. It will have no meaningful purpose, however, until more and more Christians relegate their history of politics and nation to its proper place. I'm not saying that we must ignore painful histories or even current differences of nations and culture. In heaven the innumerable crowd worshipping around the throne of God will include Irish and Northern Irish accents in joyful unison. These differences will make up the rich tapestry of eternal praise. But there is a lot of ground to cover on the island of Ireland if the church is even to begin to resemble such a mighty throng. Jesus is the Christ of God for all people. Such lordship should radically overthrow any prejudice, bigotry and hatred – be it traditional, systemic or even endemic – among God's churches. Our puny excuses based on our passports, flags and accents are not going to be accepted when the King of kings appears.

Still, we will offer a hundred and one excuses as to why we should be slow to reach out to others – if at all. The Irish don't have a particular monopoly on hating others. We might instinctively feel, for example, that the new Nigerian family who have just moved in next door are so 'odd'. They dress, talk and even smell different to us. They have different routines, priorities and values. Or we might worry that the asylum seekers who have been placed in neighbouring newly built social houses have so many issues. Would inviting them into our home even be a risk? We hope the council will move them on soon in case they even attract more crime to the area. Besides, they can't understand a word of English.

We idolise protecting our painstakingly crafted standard of living and are wary of any challenge to it from those who are not like ourselves. The fact that they might actually have been moved next door to us by God himself, so that we might have opportunity to pass on the good news of Jesus, is well beyond our consideration. However, God knows exactly how to wake us up! He puts people on our path. Those Northern Irish Christians who would probably rather die than cross the Irish border might in the end not be required to move that far at all. We must be ready to welcome everyone God sends our way. After all, he gave us the greatest and most undeserved welcome anyone could ever hope for when he invited us to a place at his table.

Denying ourselves, taking up our cross daily and following Jesus means we should be prepared to suffer in some way as a Christian. Perhaps this will mean unintentionally drawing the interest of others – our friends and neighbours – as we try to put into practice the evangelism of Jesus. It may mean we draw their anger as we welcome strangers and outsiders. They will not necessarily want the new neighbours from Africa to settle down. They won't be terribly excited if the latest wave of immigrants stay around a little longer because of our kindness. Perhaps the wider community around our church might not take too kindly when we begin to build bridges with others they perceive as their enemies. But this is the way of Jesus. He knows we will suffer shame because of him. He knows we will lose friends and possibly even family if we follow him. He is fully aware that we will be misunderstood, maligned and marginalised for him. These are the very things He went through for us. Yet it is in our suffering that he draws closest to us, and where we are conformed best to his image (Phil. 3:10–11).

Hate crimes are truly hateful, as the whole world knows. One day Jesus will come as the Prince of Peace and usher in an eternal reign of joy and delight for the entire universe. Until then, today, his people are to be visible signs of this great imminent reality. The lives we live, share and encourage one another in are meant to be reflections of what Jesus will perfect when he comes again. Let us not commit hate crime by remaining silent about this gospel reality.

Conclusion

My intention in writing this short book was not to say anything new but to practice Moses' ministry of simply repeating what the Bible says. In my sights was a very narrow band of Christian attitudes and actions. I am hopeful that for the vast majority of Christians alive today, such problems will not even matter to them. Perhaps I am being overly naive, but I would be very surprised to find the sins of materialism, careerism, sentimentalism and nationalism among my brothers and sisters in North Korea, Afghanistan or Somalia. From my perspective these are some of the more particular sins that attach themselves to 'comfortable' Christianity where the world and what it thinks is more important than it ought to be in a normal Christian's life.

Writing from within this very culture myself, I am aware that my reaction to such proclivities has been, most likely, imperfect itself. This is where the Bible needs to be our constant guide, standard and faithful friend, whose words and wounds are aimed to heal. God's word is clear and speaks about what matters most to him. If there is anything difficult, strange or unclear in our minds about these particular sins, it is not because the Bible is difficult, strange or unclear. It is simply that our minds and hearts are so twisted, blind and deaf that we need a mighty act of God to understand and think more clearly.

In the end, this book is aimed at lending more authority, authenticity and sincerity to your Christian witness. Most people reading this book are likely to come from a culture that is growing increasingly uncomfortable and even hostile towards the Christian worldview. In terms of sexual identity, the role of marriage, the sanctity of life or even Sunday trading, the average Western Christian is going to find themselves in opposition on countless fronts. However, if the world can see glaring inconsistencies between what we say we believe and how we actually live, why should anyone listen to what we have to say in relation to these big cultural flash points? Getting our house in order is so important before we venture to present a different, biblical view of the world.

We need – and the world might even respect, though not appreciate – more courage in our convictions. Fighting the materialism of our day would be no small achievement. Yet if we were to actually make it clear that this world is not our home, then the credibility of our witness would improve. Fixing our focus on being with Christ in glory is a regular battle. But if we were to find our true and most precious identities in him, instead of in our careers, we would be able to serve him, his people and his purposes much more and more joyfully. Having an eye on the particular sins that our age group is susceptible to requires a real heart of wisdom. If, however, the older generation especially were willing to hold a biblical line and winsomely raise up those who are their juniors, the future would be a lot more hopeful. Putting and keeping evangelism and mission at the top of our discipleship priorities is often unthinkable. But if we all had a deepening understanding of the true glory of Jesus, then every excuse we offer against reaching out to those different to ourselves would pale into insignificance.

Christians don't need to have caravans, careers, comforts or even a country to call their own. Christians have Christ. What we need is the courage of our convictions.

10 Publishing
a division of **10 of those**.com

10Publishing is the publishing house of 10ofThose.
It is committed to producing quality Christian
resources that are biblical and accessible.

www.10ofthose.com is our online retail arm selling
thousands of quality books at discounted prices.

For information contact: info@10ofthose.com
or check out our website: www.10ofthose.com